Où j'habite

Fiona Undrill

Heinemann
LIBRARY

Where I live

H **www.heinemann.co.uk/library**
Visit our website to find out more information about Heinemann Library books.

To order:
☎ Phone 44 (0) 1865 888066
Send a fax to 44 (0) 1865 314091
📄 Visit the Heinemann Bookshop at www.heinemann.co.uk/library to browse our
💻 catalogue and order online.

First published in Great Britain by Heinemann Library, Halley Court, Jordan Hill, Oxford OX2 8EJ, part of Harcourt Education. Heinemann is a registered trademark of Harcourt Education Ltd.

Editorial: Charlotte Guillain
Design: Joanna Hinton-Malivoire
Picture research: Ruth Blair
Production: Duncan Gilbert

Printed and bound in China by Leo Paper Group.

ISBN 9780431931241 (hardback)
11 10 09 08 07
10 9 8 7 6 5 4 3 2 1
ISBN 9780431931340 (paperback)
11 10 09 08 07
10 9 8 7 6 5 4 3 2 1

British Library
Cataloguing in Publication Data
Undrill, Fiona
Ou j'habite = Where I live. - (Modern foreign languages readers)
1. French language - Readers - Dwellings 2. Dwellings - Juvenile literature 3. Vocabulary - Juvenile literature
448.6'421
A full catalogue record for this book is available from the British Library.

Acknowledgements
The publishers would like to thank the following for permission to reproduce photographs:
© Corbis pp. **6** (Paul Seheult; Eye Ubiquitous), **9** (Emmanuel Fradin/Reuters), **11** (Royalty Free), **16**, **19** (John Van Hasselt); © Getty Images pp. **3**, **4** (Photodisc); © Harcourt Education pp. **12** (Tudor Photograhy), **20** (Jules Selmes), **22** (Martin Sookias); © istockphoto p. **18** (Mayer), **7** (Bernardlo), **7** (Berryspun); © Photodisc p. **7**; © 2007 Jupiter Images Corporation pp. **7**, **14**

Cover photograph of houses and Eiffel Tower reproduced with permission of Getty Images (Image Bank).

Every effort has been made to contact copyright material reproduced in this book. Any omissions will be rectified in subsequent printings if notice is given to the publishers.

Table des matières

Try to read the question and choose an answer on your own.

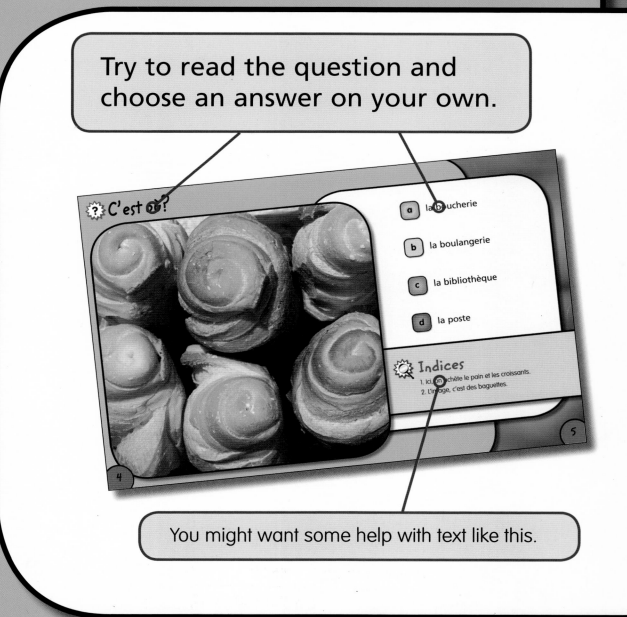

You might want some help with text like this.

a la boucherie

 b la boulangerie

 c la bibliothèque

 d la poste

 **Indices**

1. Ici, on achète le pain et les croissants.
2. L'image, c'est des baguettes.

✔ Réponse

b la boulangerie

Aimes-tu le pain français?

un croissant

une baguette

un pain aux raisins

une brioche

C'est où?

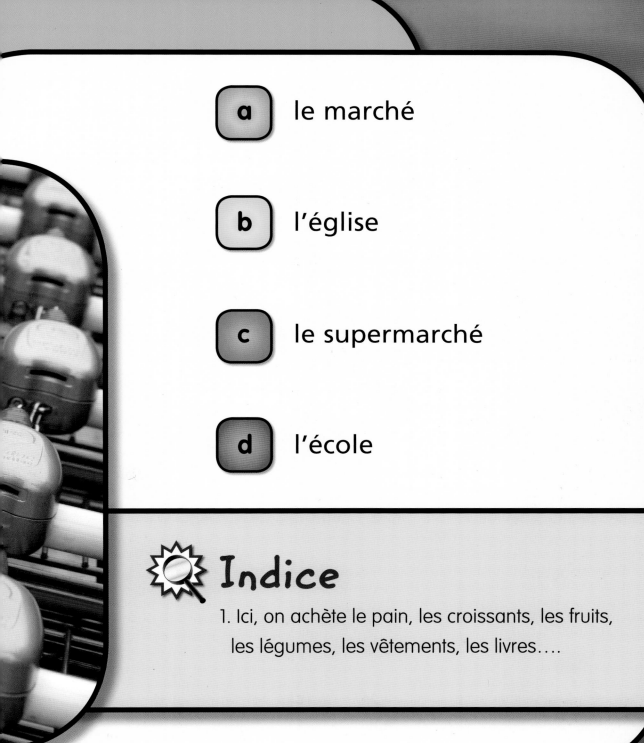

a le marché

b l'église

c le supermarché

d l'école

✺ Indice

1. Ici, on achète le pain, les croissants, les fruits, les légumes, les vêtements, les livres….

Nombre de choses différentes dans un supermarché

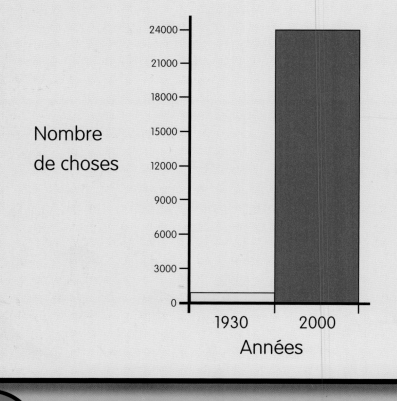

Nombre de choses

24000
21000
18000
15000
12000
9000
6000
3000
0

1930   2000

Années

10

a l'épicerie

b le café

c la bibliothèque

d l'hôtel

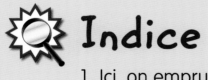 **Indice**

1. Ici, on emprunte des livres, des CD et des DVD.

☆ **Réponse**

c la bibliothèque

La bibliothèque la plus grande du monde

La Bibliothèque du Congrès
(Washington, les Etats-Unis)

Il y a:

- 128 millions de documents;
- 350 000 m² de bibliothèque;
- 850 km de rayonnages.

850 km

a la poste

b le château

c l'école

d la gare

🔍 Indices

1. Ici, on achète des timbres.
2. Ici, se trouve une boîte aux lettres.

✔ Réponse

a la poste

Images sur les timbres

- les footballeurs
- les planètes
- les animaux
- les insectes
- les trains
- les avions
- les acteurs

❓ C'est où?

Trains au départ

HEURE	DESTINATION	VOIE	TRAIN	
11.32	LE MANS	1B	16807	TER CENTRE
12.06	PARIS MP		16750	TER CENTRE
12.23	PARIS MP		862514	TER CENTRE
12.25	CHATEAUDUN		42503	GARE ROUT.
12.26	NOGENT LE RT		862491	TER CENTRE
12.34	BROU		862209	TER CENTRE
13.32	LE MANS		16751	TER CENTRE
13.41	PARIS MP		862524	TER CENTRE
14.31	PARIS MP		16752	TER CENTRE
14.32	COURTALAIN		862215	TER CENTRE

Departures / Salidas

Trains a l'arrivé

HEURE	PROVENANCE	VOIE
11.30	PARIS MP	1B
11.56	COURTALAIN	2B
12.04	LE MANS	
12.24	PARIS MP	
13.26	PARIS MP	
13.31	PARIS MP	
13.55	BROU	
14.20	PARIS MP	
14.30	LE MANS	
15.10	PARIS MP	

Arrivals / Llegadas

a la boulangerie

b le marché

c le café

d la gare

☼ Indice

1. On vient ici pour voyager en train.

★ ✓ **Réponse**

d la gare

Des trains rapides

Train	Pays	Vitesse maximum
TGV*	la France	575 km/h (2007)
maglev	le Japon	581 km/h (2003)
Eurostar	le Royaume-Uni	335 km/h (2003)

*Train à Grande Vitesse

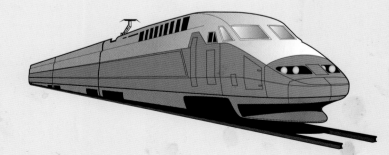

Vocabulaire